why THE GORY, BLOODY DETAILS?

An Explanation *of*
The Passion *and* The Cross

BETH JONES

Valley Press Publishers
Portage, MI

Why The Gory, Bloody Details?
An Explanation Of The Passion And The Cross
ISBN: 0-9717156-7-X

Copyright 2004 Beth Ann Jones

Published by Valley Press Publishers – A Ministry of KVFC
995 Romence Road, Portage, MI 49024
Ph: 269-324-5599, Web: www.kvfc.org

Special Thanks To: Cover Designer – Joanne Davis
Editors – Jeff Jones, Juli DeGraaf, April Wedel, Jennifer Parsons
The Person Who Sparked The Idea For This Book – Marvin Holt

Printed in the United States of America.
ALL RIGHTS RESERVED.

TABLE *of* CONTENTS

Introduction

✛

Why the gory, bloody details?

If you've seen the *The Passion of The Christ*,
you've seen the blood, the gore, the brutality.
*(If you haven't seen this movie, you've probably
seen others like it and you likely know the story.)*
Jesus Christ was graphically, brutally beaten and
nailed to a cross. One thing you can't escape
when you talk about Jesus are the gory, bloody
details and that's what we want to discuss.

The first time I saw the movie *The Passion of
The Christ*, like everyone else, I was deeply
impacted. We saw the movie before it was
released to the public when my husband and I

were at a special screening for pastors. The anticipation of the 5000 pastors could be cut with a knife and once the movie began, I don't think anyone ever moved.

Like everyone, we watched. We winced. We cried. We praised. We thanked. We wondered. When I saw the movie, my first thought was, *"Wow, this is so intense ... I wonder if Mel Gibson went over the top in making it so gruesome?"* Immediately I thought of the prediction of His Passion in Isaiah 52:14, *"Many were amazed when they saw him – beaten and bloodied, so disfigured one would scarcely know he was a person."* (NLT)

At that point, my thought was, *"Wow, maybe Mel Gibson didn't take it far enough? This is the reality. It was gory and bloody. Jesus was so*

beaten and battered that he barely looked like a
human being."

A friend of mine reminded me of a verse in
Galatians 3:1 that says, "... *right before your
very eyes – Jesus Christ (the Messiah) was
openly and <u>graphically</u> set forth and portrayed as
crucified ...*" (AMP) This certainly describes
The Passion of The Christ. What a visual!

Our generation needs this message of the cross,
this visual. We need a God-reality! We haven't
seen Jesus graphically set forth as crucified, right
before our very eyes. Not like this – not so in
our face. So, what do you do with ...

> *Jesus,*
> *His Passion,*
> *His cross?*

The Passion of The Christ, and of course,
the Bible itself – tells the real story of the cross,
and it compels us to ...

ASK SOME QUESTIONS.

Question: Some people ask the question,
"So what?" This historical figure, Jesus Christ,
died on a cross ... big deal, so what? And, the
point is?

Question: Other people ask, what makes Jesus
so different? What makes Him stand apart, so
politically incorrect, from other religious leaders?
What separates Jesus from a new age crystal or
other icons? What's the difference between
Jesus and ...

Confucius?

Buddha?

Mohammad?

<u>Question:</u> For some people, the message of the cross moves them to ask the typical, rhetorical questions – what about other religions? Why does Christianity seem so narrow-minded and intolerant? What about people in remote parts of the world who have never heard about God or Jesus? If God is so loving how could He ever send anyone to hell? Legitimate questions with good, satisfying answers. *(Though, that's not our subject in this book!)* However, sometimes, people get so sidetracked with these types of questions, they miss the point!

This is the point: the whole God-thing, the whole Christian gig is totally about the gory, bloody details. If the truth be known, the answer to this one question, "Why the gory, bloody details?", will actually answer many of the other questions people have about God, Jesus and religion.

So, with all of that said, I'd like to take some time to share an interesting conversation that took place over twenty years ago and led to my own discovery of "why the gory, bloody details."

LET'S TAKE A JOURNEY...
"Why The Gory, Bloody Details?
An Explanation of the Passion and the Cross"

Chapter *One*

✠

ONE QUESTION.

Here's my story. I have a cousin. She's intelligent. She's talented. She's gorgeous. She was a skeptic. Over 20 years ago, she and I were corresponding, actually debating a bit back and forth about the Lord. I received a letter from her one day that ended up changing my life. She wrote me a note and asked one simple question.

THE QUESTION ...

" If God is so good and God is so loving, how could He crucify, how could He murder His own Son – why the gory, bloody details?"

I thought that was a good question. In fact, I
thought it was a great question, so I set out to
write her back with an intelligent and persuasive
answer! That's when I realized that although I
knew some cliché answers, I myself didn't really
understand the answer!

I began to ask myself, *"Why <u>did</u> God send His*
own Son to the cross? Why, in fact, the gory,
bloody details?" I realized I needed to get a
clear understanding! Of course, I knew bits and
pieces of what the Bible said about Jesus and
His death on the cross. I remembered things I
had learned growing up in church.

> *I knew the songs.*
> *I knew the stories.*
> *I knew "Jesus died for our sins", but why?*

I knew He was *"the Lamb of God who takes away the sins of the world"*, but I needed it to be more than just cliché or catechism. It was apparent that before I could answer my cousin's question, I needed to "connect the dots" for myself. So, I began to pray.

✠

Like many people, I understood the basics, *"For God so loved the world that he gave his only Son, so that everyone who believes in him will not perish but have eternal life."* (John 3:16, NLT) But, why? If God so loved the world, WHY did He have to send His Son?

Was the blood, torture and hideous death really necessary?"

MAKE IT MAKE SENSE.

"Lord," I said, *"You know why the gory, bloody details were necessary. I need to know. Why <u>did</u> Jesus have to die on a cross? Why <u>did</u> You have to send your Son?"*

Have you ever asked the Lord about these things? So often we ask each other, we ask theologians, we ask ourselves – but I figured it might be best to ask God – to be absolutely honest in my approach. I continued my conversation with the Lord, *"Lord, why didn't You rescue mankind another way? You're God, why couldn't You have saved us from our sins another way? Weren't there other options? Was the blood, torture and hideous death really necessary?"*

Why?

WHY?

Why?

✦

CHAPTER Two

DO OVER.

Remember playing "Mother May I?" or "Red Rover, Red Rover"? Those were great games when you were winning, right? But the minute you lost what did you call for? A do over! Let's play again and again and again, until you win!

When it came to God's plan and saving mankind, I wondered why God couldn't say, "do over"! I asked the Lord if there were other options for saving mankind? Was sending Jesus to the bloody cross the only option?

Options?

Options? I wondered about this option. In the beginning, when Adam and Eve blew it in the garden ... couldn't God just have said, *"All right Adam and Eve, ya'll blew it. You sinned in the garden. There's obviously a flaw in the mold here, so, I'll have to do a – do over. I have to wipe the two of you out and start over."*

I asked the Lord, why <u>didn't</u> He just start over after the big fall in the garden? After all, nobody would ever know! Why not just wipe out Adam and Eve and start over with two new ones – Ken and Barbie? Why didn't God do that?

He's God,

can't He do anything He wants to do?

Options? Here's another idea that crossed my mind, why couldn't God just say, *"OK, Adam*

and Eve you blew it, so just say you're sorry –
without rolling your eyes, and then I'm going to
snap my fingers and on the count of three, we're
just going to call all this forgiven and forgotten.
We'll just start over now." Why didn't Adam
and Eve apologize and why
<u>didn't</u> God just snap His
fingers and fix it?

⊕

Why not just

Options? I thought about   *wipe out Adam*
another possibility: After
the fall of man, why is it   *and Eve and*
that God didn't say, *"Listen*   *start over with*
Adam and Eve, you blew it,
so now here's what's going   *two new ones –*
to have to happen.
                                      Ken and Barbie?

Because of your sin, you blew it for the rest of
humanity and here's what you'll have to do. In
order to be forgiven of your sins, you'll have to

7

do ten good deeds a week to get in my good
stead. If you do ten good deeds a week then
everything will be just fine and I'll consider your
sins paid for and forgiven." Why couldn't God
base the salvation of mankind on our good
deeds, on snapping His fingers or on a do over?

There's a reason
God couldn't use any of these options!

There is a really profound, legal reason which we
will explore. But before we go there, do you
concur that *if* God could have done anything
other than send His Son to die on the cross in
our place, He would have done it?

Okay, so what is the profound, legal reason?
Well, as I was asking the Lord about the various
options my pea brain had come up with, He

reminded me of Hebrews 9:22. This verse begins to tell us the reason that God sent His Son. It says, *"... without the shedding of blood there is no forgiveness."* (NIV)

Hmmmm, that's interesting I thought, but still I wondered, why? Why is the shedding of blood the chosen option for the forgiveness of sin?

As I pondered, "why?", the Lord began to lead me through a thread of Bible verses to explain it for me.

Let's walk through these passages and continue the journey.

> *Here's what we know.*
> *Adam and Eve sinned.*
> *Houston, we have a problem.*

CHAPTER *Three*

✛

LIFE GOAL.

Today, the world is a very distressing place.
People are pretty much ... Self absorbed.
Money-hungry. Self-promoting. Stuck up.
Profane. Contemptuous of parents. Crude.
Coarse. Dog-eat-dog. Unbending. Slanderers.
Impulsively wild. Savage. Cynical.
Treacherous. Ruthless. Bloated windbags.
Addicted to lust. **Allergic to God**.
(2 Timothy 3:1-2, MSG)

It wasn't always that way! God's original plan
for the world was much different. As I
continued to prayerfully seek an answer, the
Lord led me back to the beginning, to Genesis,

the first book of the Bible. As I began to read Genesis, I asked Him, *"What was it You intended to begin with – in the beginning? What was your original plan? What would have happened if Adam and Eve had never sinned?"*

As the Lord and I journeyed back to Genesis, some of the light bulbs began to turn on for me. I started to see that God really had a great plan for all of us in the beginning. It was His plan and His will to bless and prosper and fill our lives with LIFE – everything we need – a free will, a sharp mind, a healthy body, great abundance, sweet interpersonal relationships including a rich relationship with Him. God's original plan for man resounded with LIFE!

LIFE!

Genesis 2:7, says, *"... the LORD God formed the man from the dust of the ground and breathed into his nostrils <u>the breath of life</u>, and the man became a living being."* (NIV)

The picture here is simple. God scooped up some dirt and sculpted a statue. He named this statue Adam and then breathed into Adam's nostrils. God breathed *"the breath of life"* into the nostrils of a statue, and the Bible says this statue ... became a man – a living, moving, breathing person! Wow!

That gets your attention!

So, let's get the picture, God's breath fills Adam and he becomes a man full of the life of God; spirit, soul and body.

God put him in an amazing garden and gave him some instructions. *"The LORD God placed the man in the Garden of Eden to tend and care for it. But the LORD God gave him this warning: 'You may freely eat any fruit in the garden except fruit from the tree of the knowledge of good and evil. <u>If you eat of its fruit, you will surely die.</u>'"* (Genesis. 2:15-17, NLT)

We know the rest of the creation story. God created Eve from Adam's rib, and lo and behold, our great, great, great, great grandparents, to the *nth* degree, are on the planet.

These two people are full of life. God has breathed into their very being, life! He's told them to be fruitful, multiply and have dominion. He's given them everything they need for life and godliness. It was a great set up! Everything in the early creation resounded life.

Again, this is summarized in Genesis 1:26-28, *"Then God said, 'Let Us make man in Our image, according to Our likeness; let them have dominion over the fish of the sea, over the birds of the air, and over the cattle, over all the earth and over every creeping thing that creeps on the earth.' So God created man in His own image; in the image of God He created him; male and female He created them. Then God blessed them, and God said to them, 'Be fruitful and multiply; fill the earth and*

✠

God's breath fills Adam and he becomes a man full of the life of God; spirit, soul and body.

subdue it; have dominion over the fish of the sea, over the birds of the air, and over every living thing that moves on the earth.'" (NKJV)

Do you get the picture? I could see that God's whole goal, His whole desire for mankind is life. His original intent for mankind is summarized in this ...   *life, life, life, life, life, life!*
                                    life, life, life, life, life, life!

In essence, God tells Adam, *"Ok Adam, here's your home – a lush garden of pleasure – and I want you to rule it, tend it, keep it. You have dominion. I've given you authority, be fruitful and multiply, rule the garden. You're the man, Adam! But, there's this one tree: don't eat from this one tree. It's the tree of the knowledge of good and evil; don't eat from that tree because in the day that you do eat of it, <u>you will die</u>."*

God didn't want death for mankind – God only wanted life, and yet at the same time He gave man a free will with this instruction: Don't eat of that tree!

We all know the story. They ate! Remember, the Lord told them, *"... if you eat of its fruit, you will surely die."* (Genesis 2:7, NLT) Well, guess what? The day they ate of the fruit of that tree, they died.

They didn't die physically– the Bible tells us that Adam lived until he was 930 years old! (Hello?!) So, while they didn't die physically the day they ate the forbidden fruit, they did die spiritually the instant they ate! Spiritual death means "separation from God". Spiritual death doesn't mean to cease to exist – it means to be separated from God. The day they ate of the fruit – for the first time in all of creation – death entered humanity.

It's spelled out in the Bible, *"When Adam sinned, sin entered the entire human race. Adam's sin brought death, so death spread to everyone, for everyone sinned."* (Romans 5:12, NLT) Spiritual death – separation from God – spread to all men.

This separation from God, this spiritual death created that internal aching void in all of us. The Christian artists, Plumb sang about it, *"There's a God-shaped hole in all of us and the restless soul is searching. There's a God-shaped hole in all of us and it's a void only He can fill."*[1] We often try to fill that void <u>without</u> God, with addictions, relationships, intellectualism, parties, status, prestige, money and material things –

you name it. But ... we come up empty – never
satisfied – because there <u>really</u> is a God-shaped
hole, a spiritual separation called death lodged
in all of us.

Up until "the fall", mankind had been united
with God, enjoyed a friendship with Him and
lived <u>life</u> as God intended, but the minute they
ate of the fruit they <u>died</u>, and there was a
spiritual separation. Everything God made
resounded **life, life, life** – and now for the first
time death entered – it was ...   *death,*

                                         DEATH,

                                         death.

Make sense? They didn't die physically or cease
to exist, but they died spiritually, and now they
were separated from God. Their relationship
with God died. Dead.

Think of it this way: the minute they ate the
fruit, Adam and Eve stopped breathing "life"
and a "code blue" announcement went forth as
they were rushed to the figurative Emergency
Room where they were pronounced "DOA –
dead on arrival". Immediately God went to
work. His "original plan" was – life, but He also
had a "Master plan" that went into effect the
moment death entered.

> *Original Plan.*
> MASTER PLAN.
> *Gotta get life.*

---

[1] Plumb, "God-Shaped Hole". Words and Music by
Plumb. Published & Copyright 1999 by Essential
Records.

Chapter *Four*

✝

THE BLOOD.

Death seems so final. Bill was hit by a train and pronounced dead at 1am. My mom's boyfriend – young, strong, athletic – dead. I couldn't accept it. The moment I heard the news I ran to my bedroom and cried out to the Lord from the depths of my being, *"God ... No ... bring him back!!!!!"* Don't ask me to explain this theologically – maybe God gave me the gift of faith on credit – all I know is that the hospital called the house ten minutes later to say that Bill had started to breathe on his own and Mom better get up to the hospital.

LIFE OVERCAME DEATH!

Well, Adam and Eve have sinned and now humanity is dead. Death is lodged in the heart of mankind. It's not pretty. As I continued to talk to the Lord for clarification, I said, *"OK, Lord, I get it that You wanted life for mankind, but man sinned and fell and it brought death – the patient went into code blue and died – so now what?"*

As I pondered this, it seemed that God asked me this question: *"What is the only thing that overcomes death?"* I thought about it and said, *"Lord, the only thing that will overcome death is life."* Bingo!

> *Bingo!*
>
> *Bingo!*

I continued, *"So, somehow, You needed to get life back into humanity's death situation. I get it!*

Hmmmm, but where do You get life?" The
Lord led me to a verse in Leviticus, verse 17:11
which says, *"... for the <u>life</u> of any creature <u>is in
its blood</u>. I have given you the blood so you can
make atonement for your sins. <u>It is the blood,
representing life</u>, that brings you atonement.*
(NLT) Summarized, I got the idea, *"life is in
the blood."*

It started to click, I saw that when Adam and
Eve fell and death entered the scene, God
couldn't just provide knee-jerk, remedial
solutions by "snapping His fingers" or saying
"Do over!" God couldn't just say, *"Ok,
everybody just do ten good deeds and everything
will be hunky dory."*

NO.

No. God had to do something legal, intentional and eternal – something that went to the core of mankind's problem. To "snap His fingers", say "do over" or "require good works" wouldn't provide life, <u>because</u> – the life is in the blood! God had to get life back into mankind and the only place that life is found, according to the Bible, is in the blood.

If the life is in the blood, where is God going to get blood that qualifies? I wondered. Who has the blood? He, God is a spirit and He doesn't have blood. Mankind has blood, but it's been contaminated with death. Animals have blood, will that work? Apparently, for a while.

As soon as Adam and Eve fell and death entered, the Lord went to work immediately locating blood! You can almost hear the Lord saying ...

> *"Clear!"*

... as He grabs the paddles and begins to impart life, through blood, back to humanity.

After the fall, the first thing God did was to sacrifice an animal and spill its blood in order to provide a covering of clothes for Adam and Eve. *(This sacrifice typified the great sacrifice which would later be offered once for all.)*

✠

Life

is

in

the

blood!

Genesis 3:21 tells us, *"And the LORD God made clothing from animal skins for Adam and his wife."* (NLT)

Then, for hundreds of years after that, God instituted the animal sacrifice rituals as a temporary measure to provide the "shedding of blood", which would result in an atonement or forgiveness for man, which would allow God to impart "life" once again to dead mankind.

This whole process is spelled out in the Passover, detailed in Exodus 12:2-13, *"From now on, this month will be the first month of the year for you. Announce to the whole community that on the tenth day of this month each family must choose <u>a lamb or a young goat for a sacrifice</u> ... This animal must be a one-year-old male, either a sheep or a goat, with no physical defects. Take special care of these lambs until the evening of the fourteenth day of this first month. Then each family in the community must slaughter its lamb. They are to take some of <u>the lamb's blood</u> and* *smear it on the top and sides of the door frame of the house where the lamb will be eaten ... this is the LORD's Passover ... The <u>blood</u> you have smeared on your doorposts will serve as a sign.* ***<u>When I see the blood, I will pass over you. This plague of death will not touch you ...</u>***" (NLT) The blood of the innocent lamb provided protection from death.

The life is in the blood!

Remember Hebrews 9:22: *"In fact, the law requires that nearly everything be cleansed with blood, and without the shedding of blood there is no forgiveness."* (NIV) Because God so loved people He instituted this temporary system of shedding the blood of innocent animals so that forgiveness and life could be given back to man. (*This was a shadow of things to come!*)

In order to secure forgiveness each year under this system of animal sacrifices, God required the high priest to go through an extensive cleansing ritual and then this priest would be responsible for slaying an unblemished animal – a bull, a goat or a lamb.

It was then the high priest's responsibility to take the blood that had been shed into God's tabernacle – into the Most Holy Place and sprinkle this blood on the Mercy Seat, also called the cover of the Ark of the Covenant.

MERCY.

When all of this was done, an atonement – which means to pardon, to cancel or to forgive – was completed. This shed blood covered the sins of the people for one year. This blood

brought life and forgiveness to God's people for
one whole year. Each year this had to be
repeated.

ONE YEAR.

Sins Covered.

We see a more detailed description of the system
of animal sacrifices in Leviticus 16:2-25, 30-38.
(It's a long passage!) *"The LORD said to
Moses, "Warn your brother Aaron not to enter
the Most Holy Place behind the inner curtain
whenever he chooses; the penalty for intrusion is
death. For the Ark's cover – the place of
atonement – is there, and I myself am present in
the cloud over the atonement cover. When
Aaron enters the sanctuary area, he must <u>follow
these instructions fully</u>. He must first bring a
young bull for a sin offering and a ram for a*

whole burnt offering. Then he must wash his entire body and put on his linen tunic and the undergarments worn next to his body. He must tie the linen sash around his waist and put the linen turban on his head. These are his sacred garments. The people of Israel must then bring him two male goats for a sin offering and a ram for a whole burnt offering. Aaron will present the bull as a sin offering, to make atonement for himself and his family. Then he must bring the two male goats and present them to the LORD at the entrance of the Tabernacle. He is to cast sacred lots to determine which goat will be sacrificed to the LORD and which one will be the scapegoat. The goat chosen to be sacrificed to the LORD will be presented by Aaron as a sin offering. The goat chosen to be the scapegoat will be presented to the LORD alive. When it is sent away into the wilderness, it will make atonement for the people. Then Aaron will present the young bull as a sin offering for himself and his family. After he has slaughtered this bull for the sin offering, he will fill an incense burner with burning coals from the altar that stands before the LORD.

Then, after filling both his hands with fragrant incense, he will carry the burner and incense behind the inner curtain. There in the LORD's presence, he will put the incense on the burning coals so that a cloud of incense will rise over the Ark's cover – the place of atonement – that rests on the Ark of the Covenant. If he follows these instructions, he will not die. Then he must dip his finger into the <u>blood</u> of the bull and

On this day, atonement will be made for you, and you will be cleansed from all your sins in the LORD's presence

sprinkle it on the front of the atonement cover
and then seven times against the front of the
Ark. Then Aaron must slaughter the goat as a
sin offering for the people and bring its <u>blood</u>
behind the inner curtain. There he will sprinkle
the <u>blood</u> on the atonement cover and against
the front of the Ark, just as he did with the bull's
<u>blood</u>. In this way, he will make atonement for
the Most Holy Place, and he will do the same for
the entire Tabernacle, because of the defiling sin
and rebellion of the Israelites. No one else is
allowed inside the Tabernacle while Aaron goes
in to make atonement for the Most Holy Place.
No one may enter until he comes out again after
making atonement for himself, his family, and all
the Israelites. Then Aaron will go out to make
atonement for the altar that stands before the
LORD by smearing some of the <u>blood</u> from the
bull and the goat on each of the altar's horns.

Then he must dip his finger into the <u>blood</u> and sprinkle it seven times over the altar. In this way, he will cleanse it from Israel's defilement and return it to its former holiness. When Aaron has finished making atonement for the Most Holy Place, the Tabernacle, and the altar, he must bring the living goat forward. He is to lay both of his hands on the goat's head and confess over it all the sins and rebellion of the Israelites. In this way, he will lay the people's sins on the head of the goat; then he will send it out into the wilderness, led by a man chosen for this task. After the man sets it free in the wilderness, the goat will carry all the people's sins upon itself into a desolate land ... <u>On this day, atonement will be made for you, and you will be cleansed from all your sins in the LORD's presence</u> ... This is a permanent law for you. In future

*generations, the atonement ceremony will be
performed by the anointed high priest who
serves in place of his ancestor Aaron ... This is a
permanent law for you, to make atonement for
the Israelites once each year."* (NLT)

This was serious stuff.

This was involved. But, this was only a
temporary fix. It was temporary blood, from
temporary animals to temporarily provide
forgiveness and life. It was a good fix, but it
wasn't God's permanent fix. It wasn't His
ultimate plan. It wasn't His Master Plan.

What was His Master Plan?

The Master Plan is revealed. Get this: (Another

long passage worth reading!) *"The old system in the law of Moses was only a shadow of the things to come, not the reality of the good things Christ has done for us. <u>The sacrifices under the old system were repeated again and again, year after year, but they were never able to provide perfect cleansing for those who came to worship.</u> If they could have provided perfect cleansing, the sacrifices would have stopped, for the worshipers would have been purified once for all time, and their feelings of guilt would have disappeared. But just the opposite happened. Those yearly sacrifices reminded them of their sins year after year. <u>For it is not possible for the blood of bulls and goats to take away sins.</u> That is why Christ, when he came into the world, said, 'You did not want animal sacrifices and grain offerings. But you have given me a body so that I may obey you. No, you were not pleased with animals*

*burned on the altar or with other offerings for sin.
Then I said, 'Look, I have come to do your will, O
God – Just as it is written about me in the
Scriptures.' Christ said, 'You did not want animal
sacrifices or grain offerings or animals burned on
the altar or other offerings for sin, nor were you
pleased with them' (though they are required by
the law of Moses) ... He cancels the first covenant
in order to establish the second. <u>And what God
wants is for us to be made holy by the sacrifice of
the body of Jesus Christ once for all time. Under
the old covenant, the priest stands before the altar
day after day, offering sacrifices that can never take
away sins. But our High Priest offered himself to
God as one sacrifice for sins, good for all time.</u>"*
(Hebrews 10:1-12,NLT)

ETERNAL LIFE IS IN <u>HIS</u> BLOOD!

HIS!

CHAPTER *Five*

MASTER PLAN.

Have you ever played Chess? It's a great brain game because while you are making each move, you have to have a Master Plan in your mind. You have to be thinking several moves ahead in order to win. If you want to say, "Check Mate" you need to have a smart Master Plan.

Guess what? Down through the ages, with every move He made, God was working His Master Plan! His Master Plan included bringing the Lamb of God who once and for all takes away the sins of the world to planet earth!

What was so brilliant about God's Master Plan? His Master Plan would provide <u>permanent</u> forgiveness, and eternal life once and for all to everyone who would receive it. In order to provide <u>eternal</u> forgiveness and <u>eternal</u> life to mankind, God had to find <u>eternal</u> blood.

Where would He find blood that was eternal? Let's look at the options once again.

Options.

Options.

Option #1: Man – Man has blood, he's an eternal spirit being, but his blood was contaminated with death through sin and is unusable.

Option #2: Animals – Animals have blood, but their blood could not provide perfect cleansing.

Option #3: God – God is a Spirit, He's sinless and He's eternal, but He doesn't have a physical body with blood, so that's not an option. Hmmm, if only there was another option, Option #4?

Option #4: God/Man – If only God, who is sinless and eternal, could become a man so that He could have blood, then maybe that type of blood would be qualified to provide life?! Maybe that type of blood would be qualified to be shed for the forgiveness of sin. If only God could become a man.

IF ONLY!

Yes, it's true! The "if only" became "the reality"! You know the story. Although, perhaps you <u>don't</u> really know "the story!" Let's look at it with fresh eyes.

Thinking back to the beginning, the fall of man and the animal sacrifices. Hundreds of years have passed and thousands of animals have been slain to provide temporary forgiveness and temporary life for humanity.

Now, bring yourself up to 1 BC, right before the first Christmas – it's time for the continuing fulfillment of God's Master Plan!

Remember? The angel Gabriel was on an assignment from heaven to visit a young lady named Mary. The angel says *"Greetings, favored woman! The Lord is with you! ... Don't*

*be frightened, Mary, for God has decided to
bless you! You will become pregnant and have a
son, and you are to name him Jesus. He will be
very great and will be called the Son of the Most
High ..."* (Luke 1:28-32, NLT)

Can you imagine? Of course,
like any of us, Mary had a
question! *"Mary asked the
angel, 'But how can I have a
baby? I am a virgin.' ... The
angel replied, 'The Holy Spirit
will come upon you, and the
power of the Most High will
overshadow you. So the
baby born to you will be holy,
and he will be called the Son of God ... For
nothing is impossible with God' ... Mary
responded, 'I am the Lord's servant, and I am*

✠

*Aren't you glad
that Mary
wasn't some
half-
backslidden,
rebellious
young person?*

41

willing to accept whatever he wants. May
everything you have said come true.'"
(Luke 1:34-38, NLT)

I love Mary's response! Aren't you glad that
Mary wasn't some half-backslidden, rebellious
young person? Aren't you glad that she didn't
have the attitude some young people have? I'm
glad that her response was, *"I am the Lord's*
servant, and I am willing to accept whatever he
wants. May everything you have said come
true." (Luke 1:38, NLT)

Do you get the picture? God's Master Plan was
that <u>He</u> become a human being, with blood!
Eternal, sinless blood – just the type of blood
needed to legally, once and for all, forgive
mankind and give them eternal life! The life was
in His blood!

Amazing love, how can it be?
God put on flesh
and came to the planet He made.

"Though he was God, he did not demand and
cling to his rights as God. He made himself
nothing; he took the humble position of a slave
and appeared in human form. And in human
form he obediently humbled himself even
further by dying a criminal's death on a cross."
(Philippians 2:6-9, NLT)

Jesus, God the Son, chooses to step out of
heaven, humble Himself, set aside His rights as
God in order to become a human baby – to
become a human being with the eternal blood –
to live on earth for several decades knowing that
His ultimate goal had to be "the shedding of His
blood" – so that mankind could be forgiven and

injected with eternal life. He did this for you
and for me.

Now, if you'd like to stand in awe of God's
wisdom and attention to detail, let's look more
closely at the blood line.

THIS IS VITAL.

To insure that the blood of Jesus would not be
contaminated by the blood of a human mother
or father God had a wonderful plan. God, the
Holy Spirit overshadowed Mary and caused her
to conceive. In addition, God had already
designed the pregnancy process in such a way as
to be sure that the baby's blood never touches
the mother's blood! Those of you moms who
have had babies know this. For example, if a
woman with the blood type B- is pregnant, she

can carry and deliver a baby with O+ blood type! The circulatory system of the baby is never connected, other than by the placenta, to the mom's. There are two totally separate circulatory systems, thus ensuring that the blood of the baby is not contaminated by the blood of the mother.

Who thinks that was smart of God?

So, in God's Master Plan, for the first time in all of history, there is this young girl on the planet, Mary, who is carrying a baby in her womb with <u>the blood</u>! The spotless, sinless and eternal blood. The only blood that could provide eternal life! The only blood that could bring forgiveness and a fresh start for mankind.

The only blood.

Can you imagine how wonderful it must have been for heaven to watch that 9-month pregnancy? Can you picture the angels peering over the grandstands of heaven as they watched this woman who is pregnant ...

> *... with the baby*
> *... with <u>the blood</u>?!*

Now, bring yourself up to the very first Christmas when Mary delivered the Deliverer! For the first time in all of history, there is a baby – who became a child, who became a teen, who became a man – on planet earth and He has eternal, spotless blood in His veins.

The potential for mankind's forgiveness, eternal life, salvation, redemption and reconciliation is now entirely wrapped up in the blood that flowed in Jesus' veins. Imagine!

Chapter Six

THE PRESSURE.

Have you ever felt the pressure? Felt the weight of the world? Jesus did.

Now for the Grand Finale. Jesus, the God/Man, walking on the earth with this spotless, eternal blood in His veins had to live a sinless life and get to the cross. The cross was His mission. Jesus had to shed His blood for the forgiveness of our sins – our eternal life was in His blood. This was not a cake walk.

Jesus faced three extreme pressures.

EXTREME.

Pressure #1: First, Jesus, as a man had to live a sinless life. If Jesus wasn't successful in living a sinless life, it wouldn't matter if He went to the cross because His blood would be unacceptable! Jesus had to live a perfect life – as a man! Jesus set aside His rights as God and became a human being. Legally, He had to do this as a man.

If He ever sinned once, if He ever blew it once, His blood would be disqualified and all would be lost! Who knows that when people criticize you, reject you, persecute you, say false things about you and try to kill you, you could be tempted to sin? That's pressure! Jesus overcame.

Pressure #2: Second, Jesus had to lay down His life on the cross. If Jesus did not lay down His life on the cross – so that His sinless, eternal

48

blood could be spilled – then all of humanity would be lost! Jesus knew that *"without the shedding of blood"* there is no forgiveness. Jesus couldn't bail out. Jesus had to shed His blood!

The pressure was on. Just having legally-qualified-blood in His veins was not enough. Yes, He had to live a sinless life. Yes, He could never sin or His blood would be disqualified. But, ultimately His blood had to be shed. He had to choose the cross. During the last 12 hours of Jesus' life we see Him in the garden making the choice to go all the way to the cross! It was intense.

✝

Jesus couldn't bail out. Jesus had to shed His blood!

Can you see the magnitude of this?

Imagine, the eternal destiny of every person –
you and I, the generations behind us and the
generations to come – our ability to receive
forgiveness for all our sins and our ability to
have the condition of spiritual death reversed
with eternal life – hung in the balance through
the choices Jesus made in His life here on earth.

Jesus had to choose to live as a man – to live a
sinless life and to take His legally-qualified-blood
to the cross so that it could be shed for our
forgiveness!

Pressure #3: Third, if that wasn't enough
pressure – Jesus was God's <u>only</u> Son! If Jesus
didn't do it, it didn't get done. If Jesus ever
sinned once, all was lost. If Jesus backed out
from going to the cross, all was lost. If Jesus
was not successful, there wasn't a backup plan!

Jesus was not "one of the sons"; He was the only Son!

In heaven, before Jesus came to the earth, God the Father <u>didn't</u> tell Jesus, *"OK, Jesus, you're going to go first. You've got the blood that will save humanity so try to do your best, try not to sin and if you feel like it, let them crucify you. If it doesn't work out, don't worry, I've got a back up plan ... I'll just send Jim Bob, my other son, and let him give it a try."* No! The Bible says that Jesus was the only begotten Son of the Father.

You've seen it at the football games: JOHN 3:16

JOHN 3:16, JOHN 3:16, JOHN 3:16

*"For God so loved the world that he gave his <u>one
and only Son</u>, that whoever believes in him shall
not perish but have eternal life."*
(John 3:16, NIV)

Jesus faced intense pressure and He overcame.

Lived A SINLESS *Life As A Man.*

Chose The Cross – Shed His BLOOD.

The ONLY *Begotten Son.*

CHAPTER Seven

DONE DEAL.

Everybody wants to blame someone!

Some want to blame the Jews for crucifying Jesus. Some want to blame Pontius Pilate for being a wimp. Some want to blame the Romans for the brutal murder. Some want to blame Jesus' popularity and rise to fame for making rulers jealous. Some want to blame Judas for being a traitor. Some want to blame Peter for being a coward. Who's really to blame? Guess what? We're all to blame, and that's why Jesus came!

Our sins.

Jesus was here, on purpose, on a mission: to rescue all of us from sin and death. All of us.

WE ARE ALL GUILTY.

Not convinced? We need to be. Before we can really understand the magnitude of Jesus' choice to die on the cross for our sin, we need to see the magnitude of our sin! Have you ever rationalized your sin and thought, *"I'm not that bad"?* *"Sure, I've <u>sinned</u>, but I'm not a <u>sinner</u>."*

Think of it this way. God doesn't grade on a curve. According to God's grading system, if we haven't lived the A+ sinless life, we flunk!

"And the person who keeps all of the laws except one is as <u>guilty</u> as the person who has broken all of God's laws." (James 2:10, NLT)

Ever lied? Cursed by using the Lord's Name in vain? Cheated? Stolen? Lusted? Broken any of God's commandments? You're guilty. I'm guilty. We flunked. We are guilty as charged and somebody had to pay. It was our sin, guilt and shame.

Nobody took His life. He laid it down freely.

We deserved the blame, but Jesus came to our rescue. He chose to pay a debt He did not owe. Nobody took His life. He laid it down freely.

Jesus clearly said, *"No one can take my life from me. I lay down my life voluntarily. For I have the right to lay it down when I want to and also the power to take it again. For my Father has given me this command."* (John 10:18, NLT)

When they arrested Jesus He reiterated who was in control. *"Don't you realize that I could ask my Father for thousands of angels to protect us, and he would send them instantly? But if I did, how would the Scriptures be fulfilled that describe what must happen now?"* (Matthew 26:53-54, NLT)

Jesus could have bailed out at any time, but He chose to go to the cross on our behalf! We were guilty, but He took our place. Sometimes, we read the Bible and we don't realize the difficult decision Jesus had to make, as a man. He chose to go to the cross, to obey His Father, because we were on His mind. The thought of mankind being set free from the penalty of sin and death brought Jesus great joy and He endured the cross with us in mind.

"He was willing to die a shameful death on the cross because of the joy he knew would be his afterward." (Hebrews 12:2, NLT)

You know this story in the garden of Gethsemane, *"He told them, 'My soul is crushed with grief to the point of death. Stay here and watch with me.' He went on a little farther and fell face down on the ground, praying, 'My Father! If it is possible, let this cup of suffering be taken away from me. Yet I want your will, not mine.'... Again he left them and prayed, 'My Father! If this cup cannot be taken away until I drink it, your will be done.'"* (Matthew 26:38-43, NLT)

Jesus chose to drink the bitter cup! When He prayed in the garden, perhaps in our modern language the conversation would have sounded like this: *"Father, if there is any other way, if there's any other way that You can do this – if there is any other way to give mankind forgiveness and eternal life, I'd like to suggest that option. If it's possible for You to snap Your fingers and just fix this thing, please let this cup pass from me. This isn't a cup I really want to drink. If there's any other way; if I could avoid the cross; if I could avoid crucifixion; if I don't have to die and shed my blood – please let me know. But if not, I don't want my will, I want Your will. I am prepared to lay down my life – if that's Your will."*

The Bible says He sweat great drops of blood as He was deciding if He wanted to go through with laying down His life! Jesus knew what was at stake, and yet His will struggled with the final decision. The temptation to quit in the garden

was very real! Where Adam failed in the garden
of Eden, Jesus succeeded in the Garden of
Gethsemane!

Sometimes, we candy coat Jesus' journey to
the cross. Yes, thank God, He chose to lay
down His life on that bloody cross for us, but
often we don't realize that He, in his flesh,
didn't <u>want</u> to be severely beaten. He didn't
<u>want</u> to be spit at, kicked, mocked, whipped
and brutalized to the point that He was not
recognizable as a human being.

> *Jesus didn't float to the cross.*
> *Jesus chose to go.*
> *It was not pretty.*

"Many were amazed when they saw him –
beaten and bloodied, so disfigured one would

scarcely know he was a person ... He was oppressed and treated harshly, yet he never said a word. He was led as a lamb to the slaughter. And as a sheep is silent before the shearers, he did not open his mouth." (Isaiah. 52:14, 53:7, NLT)

His objective was that we have life. Jesus said, *"... I have come that they may have life, and that they may have it more abundantly. I am the good shepherd. The good shepherd gives His life for the sheep."* (John 10:10, NKJV) It's true. He did.

IT'S TRUE!

HE DID!

Jesus went to the cross. He gave His life. He was crucified. His blood was shed. In His last moments Jesus said, " *'It is finished!' Then he*

bowed his head and gave up his spirit."
(John 19:30, NLT)

Mission accomplished. What was finished? He
completed His purpose for coming to earth. The
life for mankind was in His blood! The shedding
of His blood bought forgiveness of sins and
eternal life for all of mankind. He redeemed us.
Once for all!

*"Once for all time he took blood into that Most
Holy Place, but not the blood of goats and
calves. He took his own blood, and with it he
secured our salvation forever."* (Hebrews 9:12,
NLT) Pretty wonderful of Him, isn't it?

Redeemer. Savior.
LAMB OF GOD.

In the <u>visible</u> world, He died a hideous death on that cross – people watched it with their eyes. In the <u>invisible</u>, spiritual world, what really happened? Do you have eyes to see?

The visible & The invisible.

CHAPTER Eight

INVISIBLE REALM.

The wind blows – can you see it?

So, what's the big deal? A guy was crucified.
To those watching with their <u>natural eyes</u>, they
saw an innocent man beaten to a bloody pulp,
hung on a cross by thugs. Sad, but so what?
He wasn't the first person to die by such a
hideous death.

Natural eyes.

Spiritual eyes.

Those of us today, who are watching with our
<u>spiritual eyes,</u> we see more. On that cross,
something spiritual was happening in the

invisible realm. We see the eternal balance changing. We see the penalty for Adam and Eve's sin paid for. We see life overcome death. We see Jesus' birth, life, death, burial and ultimately His resurrection fulfilling hundreds of ancient predictions. We see it.

> *Visible: The eye of the flesh.*
> *Invisible: The eye of faith.*

The natural eye could only see a bloody man, but the eye of faith saw Jesus on the cross as our substitute. A substitute takes the place of another. For example, in school, when the "sub" shows up, the regular teacher gets a life outside the classroom! Jesus, as our substitute, showed up on the cross and identified with every sin of every man, woman, boy or girl – He paid

the wage we owed – through His death, so that
we could be free to receive eternal life.

"For the wages of sin is death, but the free gift
of God is eternal life through Christ Jesus our
Lord." (Romans 6:23, NLT) He paid our wage
and we got His gift.

HE PAID.
WE GOT THE GIFT.

The eye of faith saw that His cross was our
cross, we deserved to be punished for our own
sins, but He took our place and we were
crucified with Him.

Through the eye of faith, we see that the
Passion and the Cross isn't just about <u>a man</u>
who survived beatings, mockery and torture.

The Passion and the Cross is about <u>the Man</u> who made a decision in the ...

GARDEN OF GETHSEMANE

to rescue mankind from the sin and eternal death that had plagued humanity since the ...

Garden of Eden.

Here's the real story behind the ...

gory,

BLOODY

details.

When Jesus died on the cross – in the physical world, it was blood and guts; but when Jesus died on the cross – in the spiritual world, it was life over death. This was all predicted hundreds of years before Jesus came on the scene! Listen to Isaiah's amazing, detailed forecast!

"Who has believed our message? To whom will the LORD reveal his saving power? My servant grew up in the LORD's presence like a tender green shoot, sprouting from a root in dry and sterile ground. There was nothing beautiful or majestic about his appearance, nothing to attract us to him. He was despised and rejected – a man of sorrows, acquainted with bitterest grief. We turned our backs on him and looked the other way when he went by. He was despised, and we did not care. **Yet it was our weaknesses he carried; it**

> *He was wounded and crushed for our sins. Who realized that he was dying for our sins?*

was our sorrows that weighed him down.
And we thought his troubles were a
punishment from God for his own sins!
But he was wounded and crushed for our
sins. **_He was beaten that we might have_**
peace. **_He was whipped, and we were_**
healed! All of us have strayed away like
sheep. **_We have left God's paths to follow_**
our own. **_Yet the LORD laid on him the_**
guilt and sins of us all. He was oppressed
and treated harshly, yet he never said a word.
He was led as a lamb to the slaughter. And as a
sheep is silent before the shearers, he did not
open his mouth. From prison and trial they led
him away to his death. _But who among the_
people realized that he was dying for their sins –
that he was suffering their punishment? He had
done no wrong, and he never deceived anyone.
But he was buried like a criminal; he was put in

a rich man's grave. But it was the LORD's good plan to crush him and fill him with grief. Yet when his life is made an offering for sin, he will have a multitude of children, many heirs. He will enjoy a long life, and the LORD's plan will prosper in his hands. When he sees all that is accomplished by his anguish, he will be satisfied. <u>*And because of what he has experienced, my righteous servant will make it possible for many to be counted righteous, for he will bear all their sins.*</u> *I will give him the honors of one who is mighty and great, because he exposed himself to death. He was counted among those who were sinners.* <u>**He bore the sins of many and interceded for sinners.**</u>*"*

(Isaiah 53:1-12, NLT)

The bottom line?

God's original plan for man was life, life, life! Man disobeyed God, ate the fruit and died – spiritually and eternally separated from God. Code blue, DOA. God immediately went to work and covered the sin and death with the life that was in the blood of innocent, spotless animals. It was temporary.

God's Master Plan was in progress, where He Himself – as the eternal, sinless God – would take on a human body and obtain blood that He could shed for the forgiveness and eternal life of mankind. This would be permanent.

Jesus was born – with the blood!

THE BLOOD.

He lived and He died. Nobody took His life, He laid it down freely. He endured the gory, bloody details. His eternal, sinless blood was shed and mankind is now legally given the opportunity to receive forgiveness of all sin and eternal life.

"God has purchased our freedom with his blood and has forgiven all our sins." (Colossians 1:14, NLT) Amazing.

And ... that wasn't the end of the story! Jesus rose from the dead and He is alive today! The Man, Jesus Christ resides in heaven in a glorified body with holes in His hands and feet, and He mediates between God and men. Yes, *"For there is one God and one mediator between God and men, the man Christ Jesus, who gave himself as a ransom for all men ..."* (1 Timothy 2:5-6, NIV)

On that *visible* cross, Jesus Christ became the *invisible* bridge between God and men! Death was swallowed up and eternal life was given. Oh happy day!

"Why the gory, bloody details?"

NOW YOU KNOW.

CHAPTER Nine

CHOOSE HIM.

I already knew all this! Is that what you're
thinking? Perhaps. Knowing all of this isn't the
point. It's what you do with what you know,
that is the point.

WHAT? WHY?

We've covered those.

What did Jesus do? He died on a cross. **Why**
did Jesus do it? He did it to purchase a legal
forgiveness and eternal life for every person.
This was God's ...

Master Plan.

The Lord gave my husband Jeff – a great synopsis of the Master Plan: *"At Creation, God had Christmas on His mind. At Christmas, God had the Cross on His mind. On the Cross, God had you on His mind!"*

So, what do you do with this information? The Master Plan. We've looked at the answer to, "Why the gory, bloody details?" – what now? You respond. But how? **How** do you respond?

You have to make a choice. On purpose. It's not automatic. Knowing <u>about</u> God is not the same as knowing Him, personally. Being forgiven and receiving eternal life isn't automatic. As a friend of ours says, *"going to church doesn't turn you into a Christian anymore than going to McDonald's turns you into a hamburger."* You have to choose. To

74

accept. To receive. You have a free will.

Choosing Jesus is the response
God's looking for. Jesus said,
*"I am the way, the truth, and
the <u>life</u>. No one comes to the
Father except through Me."*
(John 14:6, NKJV)

*Anyone
who calls on
the name
of the Lord
will be
saved.*

> *You must choose.*
> *On purpose.*

Your part is to respond. Make a choice.
Choose Him! Unfortunately, some people
respond with indifference. Some people respond
with unbelief. Some respond with, *"Hmmm
interesting."* Some respond with *"Ah, it's a
bunch of bunk!"* Some people have no
response, but a non-response is a response!

Others respond with childlike faith and
acceptance.

CHILDLIKE FAITH.

C.S. Lewis, Oxford and Cambridge Professor,
said, *"You must make your choice. Either this
man was, and is, the Son of God: or else a
madman or something worse. You can shut
Him up for a fool, you can spit at Him and kill
Him as a demon; or you can fall at His feet and
call Him Lord and God. But let us not come
with any patronising nonsense about His being a
great human teacher. He has not left that open
to us. He did not intend to."*[1]

Jesus said it simply, *"But to all who believed
him and accepted him, he gave the right to
become children of God. They are reborn! This*

is not a physical birth resulting from human passion or plan — this rebirth comes from God ... I assure you, <u>unless you are born again, you can never see the Kingdom of God</u>."
(John 1:12-13, John 3:3, NLT)

Jesus also said, *"<u>I assure you, those who listen to my message and believe in God who sent me have eternal life.</u> They will never be condemned for their sins, but they have already passed from death into life."* (John 5:24, NLT)

Believe. Receive. BORN AGAIN.

What is your response? Are you ready to choose Jesus Christ? Would you like to pass from death – spiritual separation from God – to life? Would you like to accept the gift of eternal life that He purchased for you on the cross?

*"He has given us eternal life, and this **life is in his Son**. So whoever has God's Son has life; whoever does not have his Son does not have life. **I write this to you who believe in the Son of God, so that you may know you have eternal life.**"* (1 John 5:11-13, NLT)

Would you like to receive eternal life and know for sure that when you die, you will spend eternity with God in heaven – a place that resounds life? It's simple.

Believe in and accept Jesus Christ. Invite Him personally into your life to forgive you of your sins and to give you **life, life, life!**

RESPOND
TO GOD.

Here's how: **"<u>For if you confess with your mouth that Jesus is Lord and believe in your heart that God raised him from the dead, you will be saved</u>.** *For it is by believing in your heart that you are made right with God, and it is by confessing with your mouth that you are saved. As the Scriptures tell us, 'Anyone who believes in him will not be disappointed.' Jew and Gentile are the same in this respect ... For 'Anyone who calls on the name of the Lord will be saved.'"* (Romans 10:8-13, NLT)

GET IT?

"Don't you realize how kind, tolerant, and patient God is with you? Or don't you care? Can't you see how kind he has been in giving you time to turn from your sin?" (Romans 2:4, NLT)

Are you willing to turn to God?

YOU CAN TRUST HIM.

Do you believe ...   YES

    that Jesus died on the cross

    and was raised from the dead by God?

Do you choose ...   YES

    to invite Him into your life personally by

    confessing and declaring

    that Jesus is your Lord?

If your answer to these questions is, "Yes", then
do it now; don't wait any longer ...

        pray this prayer outloud,

            from your heart –

                NOW...

---

[1] C.S. Lewis, *Mere Christianity*.
Harper San Francisco, 2001.

CHAPTER *Ten*

✠

THE PRAYER.

"Jesus,
I am so thankful that You
did not leave me in my sin and spiritual death.
I thank You for coming to earth
with Your sinless, eternal blood.
I appreciate the gory, bloody details.
Thank You for laying down Your life
on that cross for me.
My sins sent you to the cross.
I am so grateful that You took
the punishment I deserved,
so that I could have life and forgiveness.
You've been so kind and patient with me.
Jesus I believe in You.
I believe that God raised You from the dead.
I receive You.
Jesus, I invite You into my life and
I declare that You are my Lord.
Help me to know and follow You.
Amen."

CONCLUSION

☩

I hope this book has helped "connect the dots" for you. I can't summarize it any better than by referring you, one final time, to God's own words.

Jesus said, *"I have come that they may have **life**, and have it to the full."* (John 10:10, NIV)

*"Today I have given you the choice between **life and death**, between blessings and curses. I call on heaven and earth to witness the choice you make. Oh, that you would **choose life** ..."* (Deuteronomy 30:19, NLT)

*Oh, that you would **choose life** ...*

ACKNOWLEDGMENTS

✠

I

Simply

Want

To

Give

My

Heartfelt

Thanks

Praise

And

Worship

To

Jesus

Christ.

OTHER BOOKS BY BETH JONES

✚

If this book has been meaningful to you,
perhaps you would enjoy Beth Jones' Bible study
series, *"Getting A Grip On The Basics"*.

Getting A Grip On The Basics
Getting A Grip On The Basics for Kids
Getting A Grip On The Basics for Teens
Getting A Grip On The Basics of Serving God
Getting A Grip On The Basics of Health & Healing
Getting A Grip On The Basics of Prosperous Living

(Available at your local Christian bookstore or
through Valley Press Publishers, www.kvfc.org)

To contact the author, please write to:

Beth Jones
Kalamazoo Valley Family Church
995 Romence Road
Portage, MI 49024
www.kvfc.org

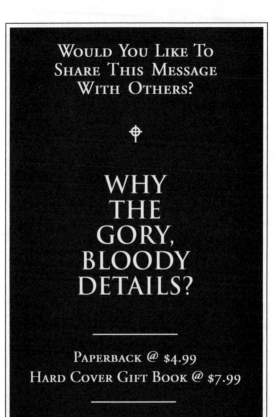